HER_A_WIN

Robin Owsley

www.selfpublishn30days.com

Published by *Self Publish -N- 30 Days*

Printed in the United States of America

ISBN: 979-8-64386-282-6

1. Autobiography 2. Addiction 3. Faith 4. Self Help

Robin Ousley *Her_A_Win*

Disclaimer/Warning:

This book is intended for lecture and informative purposes only. This publication is designed to provide competent and reliable information regarding the subject matter covered. The author or publisher is not engaged in rendering legal or professional advice. Laws vary from state to state and if legal, financial, or other expert assistance is needed, the services of a professional should be sought. The author and publisher disclaim any liability that is incurred from the use or application of the contents of this book.

Acknowledgement

"*Da'Jonna Monique* - You were the perfect person to step up to the plate.

Desmond DeAundre - You provided guidance.

Devin Anton - You were security.

Robin Daisy - You never failed to use every moment as a teaching moment.

We took so many losses in a short period of time; how can we not have leaned on one another. These four showed me how to carry-on even when everything I once knew had shattered. Those West children maintained their lives, pushed even harder every step and hid every emotion they had inside so well. I did not have a trace of them being affected in any manner from our ordeal. You guys have been through a lot at such a young age. It was as if you guys already knew the outcome would be okay! It did not dawn on me when I carried you guys for nine months each, that you guys would turn around and all carry me at such a tender age at once. Humbled to have you guys in my life. ... I birthed my angels - Them Four West Kids Mommy ***R.O***"

"I know it was not intentional and I respect the way you accepted my backlash; out of misunderstanding of what you were facing ... but ... ***Damon Sr.*** - when I ran to look for you ... that is where I found ME! Thank You. He wasn't just my children's father! He Was A True Friend! Rest Peacefully King 03/27/1977-12/03/2019 ***R.O***"

"God will flip your world upside down just to get you on the path that He created just for you ... Who must I be? To be still in my right mind ... Who must I be? To be still amongst the living ... Who must I be? To be still smiling, still loving and enjoying life with the people I love. God, you allowed me to lose myself, then to find myself again seeing that you were always there in the middle. ... ***R.O***"

TEST EVERY SPIRIT ... ***GOD IS LOVE & LOVE IS GOD***

Table of

Contents

Introduction

She's on a different kind of HIGH … ***HER_A_WIN***. The nightmare that came true was actually the key she had to use on the door created just for her. … Because sympathy was not in my plans; that did not mean I was not into understanding. My only goal left is to continue to get stronger and wiser than ever before.

"It was fine when you had no reason to quit on us …

I got beyond tired of looking for you to get better

and come rescue us, so I rescued us myself from

this nightmare … ***NOT LOOKING BACK***!"

HER_A_WIN

When night falls, fear and insecurities set in. No matter how many problems in a day's work I have solved, the return of night always seems to bring an uncertainty over me. Let me take you on a journey through the unseen nights through my lens. I wake up most days at 5:30 a.m. to give me enough time to cleanse and cover up all the silent cries that have taken place during the night. Cries of how and where I went wrong for my life to be reduced to nothing. Around mid-day, my mind is racing with millions of thoughts on how to overcome the circumstance that I am facing. There was never any real solution, it just made me panic more on my downfall.

By the end of the afternoon, an uneasy feeling starts to creep up letting me know that with all my worries and working, it is still not enough to avoid the tears that consistently run down my face during the night. After a daylong of holding it all together so the world would not detect my PAIN, MENTAL PAIN; I finally unleash the hidden uncontrollable tears that come from sadness, guilt and shame.

When I was younger, I always had this one dream that I was falling into a hole and there was never anyone there to catch me from the fall, nor was there anyone to help me avoid falling. Although this was a dream, I was of an age where I can remember it clearly and I know this dream went on for some years. I could never wrap my mind around the meaning of that dream. According to Learning Mind, when someone experiences falling in a dream, it indicates a lack of control or fear in some area of your life. It suggests you feel insecure, lack stability, have low self-esteem, or feel aimless in life. You could fear losing your job, your partner, your house, your social status, etc. Falling dreams can also suggest a sense of inferiority, shame, or feeling under pressure (htpps://www.learning-mind.com/falling-dreams).

All I could do was feel myself falling and falling, never reaching a surface then waking up frantic. As I matured with age, I can now imagine that it was a message behind those dreams, which was only going to be unlocked through time, wisdom and understanding of life. My dreams of falling usually ranged from different heights and my subconscious mind was implying that I will experience a period of hardship and poverty, falling from favor from those around me and friends around me who do not have my best interest at heart ("Learning Mind" htpps://www.learning-mind.com/falling-dreams). I was in a period of time in my life where the very least expected, the most disturbing, and the most unwarranted situation has taken place for the fourth straight year. Being of sound mind and able body, doing things right and focusing on my goals while planning for the future, my family and I became HOMELESS. How did I get to that place again? It's a great question. Let me fill you in.

Sadness

Damon and I started out as two young teenagers in love. When we met, we were at the tender age of 15 and did not bloom into a relationship until we were both 17 years of age. Damon was basically living his life as an adult on his own, and I wanted to be on my own so bad, I was not too far behind him. When we became a couple, I realized Damon was already a father of two children, a girl and a boy. As a 17-year old, with no children of my own, I felt it was unusual. Damon had explained his life story to me and it then gave me a clear understanding of his circumstances and his lifestyle. After two years had passed, I then too was with child, our first child together. We talked about having a family in the future but the future came sooner rather than later.

Our relationship was great in the beginning, but after I found out that Damon had fathered another child with his son's mother, I was heartbroken and just knew it was the end of everything. Slowly, we recovered - after all we were expecting our first child together in late June of 1997. Although I was unsure about where my life was headed, the only thing I knew was that I was creating life and was setting out to be my child's first and best role model. I was not into any he-say, she-say games and I was not into my-child, your-child. The child I was carrying, which later we found out was a girl, was going to be a part of her dad's and older siblings' life without chaos and only order.

We still had our ups and downs, but it always seemed as if it was nothing we couldn't get through. This went on through the years of me birthing our four beautiful children. I had learned to trust Damon and it was with everything I had in me; in my eyes there was no wrong he could do. No one could make me believe he was wrong or there wasn't a reason behind his actions. I was that person who was head over heels in love, and that kind of love blinded my vision to see clearly, or should I say see red flags. I do not believe anyone wants to believe that someone they were in love with for 20-plus years was falling apart right before their eyes. There was nothing I could do to stop it because I couldn't believe there was something wrong with Damon and that he had an addiction.

Guilt

During our first 13 years of marriage, Damon and my kids had become the center of my world and they were all I built my life around and knew. Things had started to fall through the cracks and our money was not adding up, but I just covered it up and handled what needed to be done. I was seeing the life I had hoped for coming together, so I emptied my thoughts of what could be going wrong and looked forward to what I wanted to happen.

The year of 2013 is when the first eviction notice came and life as I knew it started to change. I had just purchased my first dog ever, a Boykin Spaniel, and I was three months shy from graduating from Ursuline College with my BA in Legal Studies.

As one could see, I was doing well. On the other hand, Damon had lost his job of five years, but he stated he just wasn't going back to the job as a driver because they wanted him to do too much. Damon was in charge of paying all of our bills because I felt that he was the head of the house and my life was extremely busy, so I couldn't take on any more responsibility.

Damon consistently made late rent payments, which accrued additional late fee charges. This had to be going on for some time because just out of the blue, the property owner called and said they would no longer accept rent payments from us and we had to leave the property the following month, which was less than two weeks away. I didn't even have time to think of what had gone wrong, all I did was pack, work, and go to school; all the while looking for another place to stay. I had four minor kids, the dog and my husband that needed me, security and shelter.

As usual, I picked up the pieces to the life I had dreamed of that was becoming shattered and we moved on. Damon's famous words that became so familiar to us were, "We are going to make it," in hopes that it was reassuring us that this wasn't the place for us anyway. I heard his words and his excuses, but my understanding of what happened was so unclear to me. I never questioned the situation at hand; I just believed everything Damon told me. Blind faith in man had me saying, "You are right. It will be all right." Honestly, all facts and evidence were showing the total opposite. I am not totally sure if I didn't want to acknowledge it, or if I was too focused on finishing my lifelong goal of completing a college degree, to understand that something under the surface of my life wasn't right.

Nonetheless, we found another house and moved our family in. Everything was going great, I successfully completed a lifelong goal of mine to become a college graduate. I had started letting my faith in God and in myself be the course in my direction of life. I felt that paying my bills on time and having food daily for my kids to eat were my main focus at that time, therefore, a year in this new apartment was going to be good for us to stack our money and get a bigger place.

The thing about being addicted to a substance, the need to feed your habit outweighs your need to provide for yourself or your family. I have learned that when a person is hiding something, then he or she will find ways to have others not critically or independently think for themselves and gain control over the information that they tell you. I was so wrapped up in the thought that Damon will tell me any and everything, I never questioned him. I just listened to him and made up my mind that we would be okay.

What is even crazier, I had no real idea why we were having so many financial problems. When I say absent-minded, I basically was so focused on me and my needs and how I saw the next year looking like for my family that I never bothered with what was going on daily. I am a person who believes people are who they say they are, so I was blindly following a man who was blindly leading himself and his family, without a goal, plan or resources. The signs were all there, but my heart wouldn't let me put the pieces together.

Shame

My heart went into a panic, (a long cry) OHHHH NOT AGAIN, what, what, what is happening? I thought he said he had this all taken care of. If we are going to court, what happened to our three-day notice? Binggggg ... that is my defense, which is what's going to buy me more time. Being clueless to what was happening around me; I started to wonder why the office manager would always roll her eyes at me.

Whenever I talked to Damon about it, he would say, "Oh, she is mean to everybody." Whenever I asked him about his half of the rent, he would always say, "Oh, she said I can pay her this amount until the next time." In the back of my mind, it didn't sound right, but again I trusted his every word. I just so happened to have an off day in the middle of the week and just when I decided to sleep on the couch and not go out of the house that day, someone slid something underneath my door.

I thought it was a note stating building maintenance business or something, but I couldn't rest until I figured out what it was. While lying on the couch, I had an uneasy feeling for a while; deep down in my soul I just couldn't put my hand on it. Sure enough, it was our court documents telling us we had to leave the premises and our court date was in a week. I have kids, this can't be my life. I am trying, Lord, what am I doing wrong? I broke down in tears. The feelings of loss, anger and humiliation were raging inside of me.

It was like I was screaming silently, "What am I doing, Lord, to deserve this again?" It seemed as though my faith and understanding in who God was and who I was, was leaving. I was crashing slowly, but in the way back of my mind I knew it was a test and it had a purpose.

For some strange reason, I never wanted Damon to see me cry over our problems and how they really bothered me. I think I wanted him to know I had faith in him and believed he would never put me and his children in these crazy predicaments. I actually would prepare a script to myself, so when I would ask him what was taking place again, I wouldn't sound like I lost all hope and faith in him. Later that night Damon come home, and as I brought this matter to his attention, his response was outrage. He acted like he and the apartment manager had worked out this matter, and this had to be a mistake. Damon assured me this would be taken care of Monday morning.

When one is great at controlling someone's mind, they know just what to say so one can believe every word they say. After Damon spoke his authoritative words, I believed him and thought nothing else about it during the course of that weekend. Monday came, and I told Damon to take care of this matter with the property manager and I headed out and would be back later. Disappointment came along with the lies.

Something in my soul started to question Damon, my soul started to feel uneasy around him. Something deep down in my soul wouldn't allow me to keep believing it was the properties we were staying on being the problem. I was so accustomed to picking up the pieces and avoiding the underlying situation I had told myself everything from, maybe Damon was taking care of another family to that maybe he really hates me and is out to destroy me. It never dawned on me that his habit was a greater need for him than taking care of his family. He was addicted to alcohol and that was a monster I was facing head-on. From lies to wasting finances, this monster came STRONG.

It was now the day we went to court. We arrived at the courthouse early as we sat in our car preparing for the worst, but also preparing to tell our version of what had taken place. Nothing was even clear to me. All I knew was what Damon had told me and he stuck to his story the entire time. Therefore, I was relying on my defense that we never received a three-day notice to leave the premises. Both parties arrived, facts were presented, and come to find out, she took all steps that were necessary to evict a resident on their property. We had three days to leave the premises - that didn't include the weekend that was approaching. I was never told anything, not even an "I am sorry for putting you through this again." Damon watched me cry and pack for three days. I had millions of thoughts running through my mind, but Damon said nothing. He never tried to assure me that things would be alright, he never tried to assure me that he had a plan, and he never ensured me that everything that took place was a bogus lie.

I had no place to call my own, but it was truly a blessing for me to have a sister who also had a family and children of her own. She never hesitated to open up her doors for me and my children. My family and I then returned back to my older sister's house. Everything that took place happened so fast, even when the judgment was set and in place, it was still unclear to me what happened, and what I was to make out of my life next. I am not the type of person that lets sadness, guilt or shame take over me, and I refuse to become content in my brokenness. Therefore, I pulled myself together rather quickly this time around. I reinforced a schedule that would work for my children because the need for us to stay productive was so much greater than ever before. Finally, my concern for Damon was at an all-time low.

Stable Enough to Keep Moving

Being without a place of my own for those next five months, I realized finding a place to reside was not easy and took major time. After working countless hours and saving the majority of my earnings, I finally found us a new place to reside. I was going through so many emotions I couldn't place any of them in order. Even though, that was an extremely hard place for me in life.

I still had to somehow help my children to understand what had taken place again, and to understand why we had to leave our place so suddenly and return to their aunt's house. Damon was at the point where he gave us no help financially nor did we receive mental support. He had become more and more complacent in his drunkenness so that in reality, he had no real clue of what was going on or where his children and I were on a day-to-day basis. I tried so hard to be of a stable mind for my family and to put us back together. I knew this was going to take time for me to heal, in order for me to be whole again, and be both mom and dad and get my family back stable. At that moment all I was concerned about was getting my daily routine back to when our days were normal.

Alcohol had altered Damon's cognitive thinking process. One would think a husband, father, and man would be doing everything in his power to bring his family back to a loving, caring, thriving home life; that was not the case at all. While I, the mother, was in complete disorder mentally, I was doing everything in my power to get my family back to order. Damon, on the other hand, was running around in the streets as if this situation that we were facing was normal and life was just as he liked it.

When I become under a lot of pressure, I do what I know how to do, work and work some more. I spent my afternoons and nights working; during the day I would look for places, but finding a place was hard because by this time our name was in the system for being evicted, so finding a place was like having slim to no chance. A good friend of the family had just moved into a nice home in South Euclid, and I talked to her about moving there. She put in a good word for us to her landlord and we were able to move in late November. The thrill of having my family all together and whole again was all I thought about. I was more concerned about having my family whole again, not paying attention to the fact that I came up with the bulk of the rent plus deposit on my own. It did not send a red flag that I was doing this all myself and that it was a huge burden I was taking on, but all I knew is that I wanted my family by any means.

Notes

Focusing

Although we had signed a 12-month lease in November, on a place to call home, we continued to stay with one of my sisters until after the holidays, in January. We had completely moved in our place, structure was in place and a balance of how things were going to go was in order. Life was beginning to be one of normal living habits and everything felt as if it were going as planned.

Our children were enjoying their new house, the dog had a yard to play in and long streets that we would walk him on daily, and Damon even seemed content with the place. I started to understand that I had to collect the money for our rent from Damon in order for it to be paid and on time. That is what I had told myself was going to happen this time around. I was losing trust in him, but I didn't tell him. I just did what I usually do, allow my actions to be my voice. Damon would allow me to believe that he was handling business and be doing the total opposite because alcohol had a stronghold on his mind so that he never saw anything wrong with his actions.

Matter-of-fact, he would always say, "They (meaning the property owners) can wait. I will pay them when I get it." The business side of me kicked in this time which allowed my mother and me to have a great system of paying the landlord. I would collect his portion of the rent and I always had mine, then I will give all the money to my mother because I was at work during the day, and she would get a money order and meet the landlord and pay him. This went on for five months, then one day out the blue, Damon said to me, "Why does your mother have to pay the rent? I can do it."

Not thinking clearly, I said to myself that maybe this is one of the ways he feels like he is the man of the house and that he has some control over what is going on.

See, I always thought if I let Damon be the man and lead his wife and family, then he would do just that. I had unexplainable faith in this man. I told my mom that Damon said he would pay the rent to the landlord from here on out. I thought he was finally stepping up and I really had faith that he was going to pay the rent on time and in full. My mother even tried to warn me that is what he would always say, that he paid the rent the other times and look where it got you. I would brush it off like she didn't know what she talking about. All I could say to myself is that he wouldn't do us like that again; he has seen how hurt his kids and I were. Months went by, I heard less and less from the landlord, so I believed my life was in order and our bills were being taken care of.

Working two jobs full-time and part-time, the only thing on my mind was getting ahead and staying ahead. Damon worked a part-time job in the evening but all he seemed to talk about is how they would get drunk on the job. I pushed my idea of him finding something else, that is not a great idea for a workplace when you are trying to stop drinking and getting your life together.

One day – I remember this so clear – things started to unfold. My neighbor saw how I was going from one job to another, working day in and day out.

She stopped me in the driveway as I was pulling out headed to work and said, "Robin, Damon and two more people sit on this porch all day and drink every day."

I responded, "He said he doesn't drink with them and he has been trying to get another job daily."

She said to me clearly, "I am tired of looking at it, it hurts me to see them drinking like they do."

That sat on my mind all night while I was at work.

I thought, "He drinks all day, then all night at his job, and still tries to come in my house at 12 a.m. like he is a teenager. This is an adult man with kids."

I knew this was going to be a tiring morning because I was ready to confront this situation.

Notes

Readjusting

The last time I would ever put effort into loving my husband of 20-plus years was that day. The day my life would never be the same. I came home as usual from my night shift job. I gathered my blankets and pillows and slept on the couch that morning because I wanted to make sure Damon did not leave out before I said something to him. Mentally, I was drained and prepared to tell him all he needed to hear.

When I am stressed, I cannot really sleep well, therefore a couple of hours passed and I slept really well, but around 9 a.m., my body woke itself up and I knew things were going to get bad. Damon came down the stairs as usual on his way outside, going nowhere.

I stated, "Where are you going? We need to talk."

Damon said, "Talk about what? I have something to do."

Then, I did not even beat around the bush. "So, you mean to tell me you drink with the neighbors all day long, while I am at work, then turn around and go to work all evening and drink there? You have been staying out till 12 a.m., running around like a teenager; you are a husband, father and a grandfather. When are you going to grow up?"

He went off. Everything was a lie, who I received my information from did not know what they are talking about, and my favorite line, "You are not my mother or anyone to me. I don't have to explain shit to you. "

I noticed there was always a pattern of him telling me he didn't have to explain anything to me. I always felt like I had a voice and what I said mattered.

As I am looking back, my voice mattered when it was put to use for the good of everyone around me, but it needed to be silent when it came down to how others made me feel. That morning was when I saw something unusual come from Damon.

Over the years we had our moments that were not pleasant, but that moment took me on a spin.

He had rage and revenge in the tone of his voice when he said to me, "I will spit on you. I don't give a fuck about you, and who are you that I have to answer to." It was different. I stated, "I am your kids' mother, your wife."

I was sitting in my chair, he was standing over me and his friend was in the car waiting on him to come outside. His friend walked into my house, without knocking, and said, "Come on, let's go."

Damon looked at me and said, "Fuck her. She don't mean shit to me."

Everything I felt for him, everything I tried to be in his life, left my soul that day. I knew it could never be the same. I was drained mentally and physically, but

I picked up the pieces to my life and kept on moving. I cannot even recall how he came back. But more than likely he said it was all my fault and I believed him. One thing I have learned is I didn't have to investigate too hard, God had placed proof in my path so I did not have to question Damon on anything - the proof was there.

My shift was changing. I was going on day shifts, so Damon already had a pattern of staying out till 12 or 1 a.m. I did not say anything. The landlord finally got in contact with me, told me how disrespectful Damon was to him and his father and how he tried to work with him but he refused to do business with him any longer. I asked Damon a little bit concerning that, he then accused me of sleeping with the landlord. Then he questioned me about confronting him concerning another man. I left the entire situation alone because I realized I could not reason with a fool. I tried to rectify the situation concerning the house payments, but he had put me too far in arrears and I did not have thousands to try to catch up.

I refused to live in fear, guilt and shame with this man any longer. I went to court and had to move, but I finally realized that Damon had a serious problem. My husband was an alcoholic and he was not only taking himself down, but I was going fast with him.

Notes

Notes

Shifting

I never looked at another man in the 20 years when Damon and I were together, I didn't know what to really think or say. One part of me was glad this situation I was in was going to be over, another part of me did not want to let go. I have a hard time letting go ... so I stay longer attached to people who damage my heart.

As I said, this eviction was sad, but I figured it was what I needed to move on with my life. Homeless again for the third time in three years, the four children and I packed our things to move into my sister's house again. I think Damon knew in his spirit that I wasn't planning on moving again with him. He knew how he treated me, he knew once I became silent about the situation and didn't even cry over the eviction, he knew he had lost me. The next morning, Damon and I took our children to school and we rented a truck to move our belongings to storage, Damon opened up to me, he cried like a baby on how he didn't understand how things went left with us, how he needed me and the kids and please don't leave. He promised he had a plan.

After so many years, I knew this was an attempt to get me back to being under his command. I did not fall for it, because words meant nothing to me coming from him anymore, I needed to see actions. He rented hotel suites for us this time around, and he went to the extent of getting a place within four months' time. He even put his name on the lease since my credit was damaged from previous evictions.

The kids and I stayed at my sister's house, Damon stayed with one of his family members. It was not what I expected, but I had peace. My focus was to go to work, and work on me. During this time, I started figuring out me again. My attachment for him was fading and my drive to survive came back. I was working and saving;

this time I felt like I should take my time finding what I needed and not something I was forced to move to.

Learning new ways to love myself, I had begun losing weight by exercising daily, studying to get in an MBA program, working on meeting different people and just really living. My focus was no longer Damon and his daily habits because I was trying to become whole again while processing all that I had been going through. As time went on, his anger toward me became more prevalent.

Damon's dependency on alcohol started to cripple his ability to even function at his evening job. He started coming up with so many excuses concerning his employment. Little did he know I was aware of his excessive drinking. I would find so many empty liquor bottles hiding in the bedroom closet. Damon thought he had convinced me that he no longer used alcohol. Finally, it was no longer excuses concerning his drinking. He started verbalizing how he was a grown man and he could do what he wanted to do; plus he verbalized that I was not his mother.

God knew that I was dealing with too much, my spirit was broken and all I wanted to do was run away and never come back. I couldn't believe that I had put myself back in this situation, but he told me he had changed, was what I kept telling myself. All I had been doing was speaking empty words to him. Then on the other hand, I actually stopped caring so much about him or his whereabouts. My only focus was to work more hours and save money because I was determined to move out of Damon's apartment. I couldn't take any more arguments over nothing anymore.

I couldn't stand to hear, "This is my house you can leave," anymore; or when Damon would say, "I will do for you guys when I want." I had enough and my mind was made up.

This is Not My Life

I wasn't paying attention to my past financial hardships until one day my past unresolved circumstances showed up at the most unexpected time. It is said that when it rains it pours, and I was not prepared for this new storm. The paycheck that I received just a few days away from us leaving to go on my trip had gotten garnished. I was now trying to convince Damon that it was time for him to step up and pay more on the rent because the garnishment did not allow me to pay my part of the rent in full.

Thinking back, I knew I was dealing with a person who did not have it in his character to get a job and do what a man is supposed to do, be the provider. He did not want us to go and he knew he wasn't going to do anymore to pay more on the rent, seemingly we were behind anyway; he is the only one who knew that. I decided to go on our paid-for trip in hopes that my current situation with my job would've gotten through to him, but his mouth spoke one way, and his actions told the truth.

When living with a spouse on whom alcohol has a stronghold, and trying to raise four children, one cannot save and have money on standby. I had been literally living from paycheck to paycheck and when that garnishment on my paychecks was applied, I felt stress in a whole new wave. I asked myself, how can one person take care of four children and a household with garnished wages? It was impossible to live life with garnished wages, and no help from my spouse.

You somehow know when your back is up against the wall; that is when you can really find out who you have in your corner. I can really say God carried me literally. At this point, after four years of the same cycle, I became unclear of my own today and future. Every time I would bring the financial situation up to Damon he would say two things. "You work a full-time job" and "What about the money you are saving to move out with? Use that."

It seemed as if I had depleted my ability to keep going and for sure my savings. Then I remembered I was paying a legal plan through my job. So, I filed for BANKRUPTCY. I was working with nothing, so I was not scared to take that leap of faith. I obtained a lawyer, paid the legal fees to cease the garnishment to get my life somewhat back in order.

I knew that I was an educated woman and this is not where I should be in life, so filing for bankruptcy was the hardest thing to do. It was also the most rewarding thing in my life since my college graduation. I said hardest because I was so used to depending on Damon or my mother for everything that went on in my life, so when I had to obtain a lawyer and make an appointment to go see him, it was so scary for me. I felt I had to grow up with all that was already going on in my life. I was waiting and waiting for Damon to show up and rescue me, but he never showed up.

I knew all this had to be done, as my life was being taken away from me in front of my very own eyes. I was alone and scared, but becoming whole and gaining freedom. That was one of the most amazing feelings I had experienced in the last few years. I was witnessing my old life die away while giving birth to my new life.

One morning as I was going on about my day, I told Damon that we needed to talk. I explained to him, that I was fully aware that he had an addiction problem and it was time for him to get help. I told him these last four years had set us back 10 years and had destroyed everything we had built. He listened, cried and told me it was time for him to get help. As I know now, when a person wants help is when a person gets help. He was very clever and spoke to my itchy ears. See, as I quoted for years on my social media sites, "Our eyes can only see what our minds are prepared to comprehend." For many years I saw it as one way, but now I understand that I too could not comprehend that my husband of 15 years was fully addicted to alcohol. That is why I could never see the signs, the many signs, I COULD NOT SEE THEM.

A million thoughts raced through my head during that period of my life. All I would say was it was all my fault. I would say that because I accepted Damon drinking daily and not ever helping him set limits. I would always be willing and always available to give him hundreds of dollars at a time.

Even though I had no clue what he was doing with the money when he said he needed it, I gave it to him. I had blind faith in him, I believed everything he said, therefore, I would be so given to all his requests. He knew it too, so he would ask knowing I would say yes, and he also knew it hurt my heart to tell my loved ones "no." I can beat myself up a million times for being so giving, having so much compassion and trusting way too much, but it is a gift and I will carry that with me wherever I go. I feel sorry for the people who use and abuse an honest, loyal person; they suffer knowing they will never get back someone like that again in life.

Fade-Away

My life went bankrupt, everything we worked hard for went away over a four-year period. I remember the day when I found our first house in the Heights and it was moving in day for my family. We had been staying in the urban city of Cleveland for so long it felt like we were the Jeffersons when they were moving on up. Our neighbors were sad to see us go but they also knew it was necessary. We had everything we wanted. A beautiful home, well-mannered children (two boys and two girls), a faithful, loving marriage, and God even saw fit to give us the most amazing dog ever – our LBD, little brown dog, Boykin Spaniel. It was picture perfect and I couldn't ask for anything else.

I am always reading, but it was one quote that stuck, years after my nightmare had become my reality, and it said "the best quality to have is to read, to read PEOPLE," author unknown. I am constantly watching and studying people, but I never thought I would have to watch and study my husband. Damon helped me conceive four amazing, talented children and the title of being his wife. I believe he was so used to being in control of things in his life and I would always be there to catch him if he fell, he really thought that he had control over his drinking.

I understand now that alcoholism is a disease and one needs real help to overcome it rather than winging themselves back into society. I never thought it would happen to me, even though all the signs were there. I didn't want to believe a young man so strong, so dedicated to his wife and children would allow substance abuse to overpower his life.

How did I figure out that it was a problem? Damon has never been a person who was very open and always smiling; he would have to have loved and trusted you completely to allow you to see that part of him. He was never the one to make up excuses. I first noticed that he was getting in car accidents on his driving job and when he would go for drug testing his alcohol level and blood pressure would come back extremely high. His job at the time would always tell him to take a few days off then take the alcohol level test again and if he passed it he could go back to work.

Damon drove for this company for five years and once he got comfortable he started doing what made him comfortable. As the years went on, he was having more on-the-job accidents, including a few non-driving ones. I did ask him if he was drinking at work, and he said, "Yeah, but everybody does it and it's not a big deal." In actuality it was. If you are working a nine-to-five job, five days a week, you shouldn't be drinking any alcohol during those times. As well, his need for having alcohol would not have been so great. He had started buying beer and liquor to have every night when he came home, but what he didn't always mention was he was drinking on the job all day too. I researched how long it takes for the body to rid itself of alcohol and be prepared for the next day. Let's just say, with all his intake on alcohol, he was NEVER SOBER.

Awareness

Once I realized he was never sober, I knew he was always going to be an angry man in my presence. Whenever the suggestions of him to stop drinking arose, he would verbally attack me, trying to belittle me, like me bringing him truth and facts was belittling him. I don't like to have arguments – it would tear a part of my soul away because as I am telling someone about my concerns about their actions I always become the target.

I knew more than I told him, but I always felt that he would be able to handle it. I had a little knowledge concerning alcoholism. My Uncle Lewis was one, and he passed away in his early 40's while I was a teenager. All my mother told us, her children, was the doctors said that my uncle was so chemically dependent on alcohol that he was going to die if he had it or didn't have it. That was a scary message to hear as a teenager and it stuck with me for a lifetime. I couldn't see Damon at that point, and I didn't want him to get there, either.

I continued to work on my degree in Legal Studies, I continued to work day and night at my nursing job, I continued to keep my children busy with their academics and athletics. I made certain I was always on the go because that is one way I deal with pain and hurt. I had pain and hurt because I couldn't believe the man I met at 17, fell head over heels in love with and had blind faith in would not listen to my voice of reasoning and that alcohol was all he could see.

In the beginning when I began noticing the problem, I would read a lot concerning his drinking. I was going to Sunday worship every Sunday, the children and I. The men of the church would always ask, "Where is your husband? Tell him we want to see him one Sunday." He was overly possessive over me, now that I realize it, it was because he knew I deserved better. Therefore, I would take pen and paper to Sunday Service and write down key points then go home and tell Damon what I learned in service that day.

He was very clever when I would express how I tired I was of living in the dysfunction. He would say that he wanted to learn God's words with me, and ask if I could read the Bible out loud to him. His excuse was he liked listening to me read, that I had a great comprehension and could break it down for his understanding. I thought that would be an excellent bonding time, but little did I know that only lasted a few days just to get me back occupied with my life. As I sat in Sunday service year after year, I finally realized that I wasn't there to bring ideas back to Damon, I was there because I needed the messages to carry me through this STORM I was about to enter.

When I went to worship on Sunday, two things took place; the message was geared toward me and I understood it. I was under the impression that I needed to go because I had to receive this message for Damon, when all along the message was for me. I was headed into the biggest battle of my life and I had to be prepared mentally. I took notes, yes I carried pen and paper to service, then during the week I would study what was taught and it helped me to ignore Damon and his drinking habit. My home life was draining me, but week after week my soul was getting the supplements it needed to face another week.

See, when I started ignoring Damon I noticed that he was reverting back to his teenage days. He stayed out late, and when he would come in he would be extremely drunk. He used to do stuff to start arguments and accused me of sleeping around.

It hurt because I was a faithful, loving and caring wife; was an excellent mother and all I wanted was a healthy, loving family. Alcohol can come in and destroy someone's mindset about you. That is why I stayed in the Word of God. It healed me before damage from mental abuse could set in. Whenever I would say I am leaving I can't take this any longer, Damon would say, "Nobody will ever want a woman with four kids," and he would say, "Plus, you are fat and have a smart mouth."

I was heavier than I ever been before, but as I was studying the word of God, studying my coursework, I also started studying about healthy ways of living. See, pain motivates me, I take criticism concerning me, for a chance to make the changes needed for my own life. I cannot do anything about having four children, but I can do something about my weight.

I was never interested in finding a new relationship, I was more interested in getting out of the one I was in, becoming whole again and living free from seeing alcoholism. I was extremely attached to Damon, nothing he could say or do was ever wrong.

Getting Out

It was not until 2013 when I finally realized that if Damon did not put a final cap on his drinking then the future for us was going to be no more. For about three years straight prior to 2013, when I would attend Sunday Worship, the message always concerned putting man/woman before God, doing that will cause a removal of them from one's life. There was never a service I didn't receive some kind of message.

It was not until I had gone through the situation at hand and overcame victoriously that I would see the previous message that was given to me clearly. The message that I would always receive instructed me not to put anyone in front of God. I did exactly that. Damon came before anyone and anything. My biggest misunderstanding was trying to do God's work. I thought I could stop him from drinking and help Damon become whole again, but that was actually up to God and Damon.

Alcohol is one strong substance to be up against, what I am saying is people who are alcoholics can be ridiculously mean in the morning, that is why they have to get a fix early. I never understood why someone would want beer in the morning for breakfast instead of a home-cooked meal. I never saw anyone do that, so I told myself that was just the way he was. Damon ate a whole lot in the afternoon and late nights, so when he was vomiting every morning I assumed it was because he did not digest his food and he went to sleep on all he consumed. Yes, that was true but he also was drinking beer and liquor all during the day.

One might ask how I could have been so blinded by the facts. I never had to witness abuse or alcoholism in my life. Therefore, as my reality was playing out before my eyes, my knowledge and understanding of alcoholism were growing.

I considered myself as the perfect housewife, I did everything I was asked of and more. Damon was so proud to have me and show me off. He would brag to everyone about me and all that I was doing in my life. No matter what I did, no matter how wonderful of a mother and a stepmom for all his children I was, no matter how I went overboard at being an excellent daughter-in-law and sister-in-law, that wasn't enough to keep Damon from drinking.

The more I tried to build a loving, healthy family, the more he would drink. I was building and his alcohol addiction had him subtracting. When I would calculate how much money he spent on alcohol in a day, week or month his response would be, "Well look at how much you shop." My shopping became a problem because I had four children and instead of washing 15 loads every weekend, I would buy new stuff to avoid washing. That is not an excuse but that is what I used to do. I am not going to lie, Damon would always come back with facts, therefore, I learned you cannot argue with facts, you can evaluate, make changes, and do better. I never understood why he couldn't have seen my facts concerning him that way.

Sometimes I wondered if it was how I presented the facts to him. I have been told it is the way I say things, but I also know most of the ones who say that are also the ones who say I think I am this or that, including Damon. Therefore, it is not how I said things, it was the person who was saying stuff that he could not receive anything from.

When you have grown older with no clear vision of life, and you taught yourself all you have known then one can never receive any messages from others concerning them. I was once that person, but now I know better. I am always open to ways that will help me create an even better me. I am pretty sure his upbringing played a huge part in the choice to revert to the use of alcohol for every solution in his life, so my words, which may have been true, didn't feel as good as the alcohol he used to cope with life.

Therefore, my voice was to him a distraction to the source that fixed his pain. I couldn't really understand that back then, but I clearly understand now that I had to be removed from what God was going to allow to happen in Damon's life. Yes, it will and did affect me too, but God equipped me for the transition that was about to take place. While we were experiencing hardships in our lives, I was gradually letting go of Damon and gradually finding myself and my own strength. I may not have had enough resources to financially keep us from drowning, but I had enough to keep us afloat and enough knowledge and wisdom to keep working and moving forward; trouble doesn't last always!

I was so uncomfortable, with my lifestyle it forced me to see the bigger picture that if Damon didn't get any help, my life was going to keep getting worse. The year of 2012, my vision of what was taking place was not so clear, we got evicted, had time to pack and had a new place in less than a month. We moved in these apartments out in Euclid, Ohio, it felt like a box, for $750.00 and all I did was suffocate. He had every excuse why he couldn't come up with his $325.00, so my excuse for that was I didn't want to be there, no way, and he said it is going to get better, but we were once again evicted and this time I had a garnishment against me.

Damon and I rented a house in South Euclid. I figured two adults should be able to pay $900.00 a month, but when one of the adults has an unresolved dependency on alcohol that was not going to happen. I just kept feeling like I was losing more than I was putting out. I was renting furniture that I couldn't afford, struggling trying to buy food for my kids and the whole time Damon just seemed content with everything.

Therefore, we got evicted once again in 2013. We had time to pack, but this time it took us three months to find a new place. We moved what we could into storage and the rest we threw away. I kept telling myself I would replace it, it was just stuff. Yes, it was stuff but it was my stuff. Again, I compromised my own happiness because I had that much faith in Damon and we lost so much of our life in the process.

My name had two evictions against it so I explained to Damon he had to use his name. I was hopeful but no longer naive. We talked about him getting help, he knew it was a problem, and I told him this last move was going to be the last time. He promised and we moved again to Richmond, Ohio with the little stuff we still had. It was no surprise when we were back out on the street. I once had visions that if I did not get out of my situation that I would end up dead.

This man was drinking and passing out in the middle of a rage. I was not about to work hard and pay rent to a place where I didn't feel safe. I had no choice when I moved into that apartment with Damon. That was the last situation I needed to be in so I could see clearly that I didn't belong in that life anymore. I was out on the streets again. This time I knew it was over. All I had left with me were my children my clothes, my children's brand new beds, and all our pictures. I left the ones of him and me together, hoping they would explain to him that his habit was more important than us and his children.

Becoming Whole Again

I left with nothing, Damon watched me and our children struggle to move out in one car, then after everything was moved out he decided to help tie my children's beds to the top of the car. I was ashamed of myself for allowing my life to be reduced like that, but if it had not gone that way, there is no telling where my life would be now. I was going through pure HELL in the inside of me. I was in and out of eviction court, bankruptcycourt, and picking up extra shifts, so I could be prepared for my next move. Then, I'd spend my mornings calling places and putting in housing applications.

Places kept turning me down because of my previous evictions. I even tried to go get help from my local county agencies with new or used appliances, but they turned me down. I literally was told by my local government agencies that I had to be living in the homeless shelter, had some kind of substance abuse or have my children taken away from me. I was a working mom of four, who allowed a man with alcoholism to destroy everything we built, and all I was looking for was a chance to start over. I did not want money, clothes, or food, and they said no.

My family was torn apart, everything I had was gone, but I had hope and faith that if I kept pressing forward something was gone turn around for me. My sisters opened up their houses for me and my kids along with my mom. That alone gave me the ability to really get myself together. I actually learned how to save, buy things I really needed when they were on sale, and have a daily plan.

I knew that my new journey was going to be one I would be doing by myself. I was working nights and picking up extra shifts. I knew my children were at my sister's house all the time, so I paid her $250.00 a month, plus I went grocery shopping for all the children. I was saving the rest of the money because I knew my end goal was to move into our own place. I had no real clue of where that was going to be, but I did have one place lined up, from my sister-in-law. Somehow, the move-in process was becoming too long of a wait and my family was getting frustrated with my living arrangements. I don't take things people do or say to me to heart, I just learned that having your own is the only thing that matters.

Out of the blue, my brother-in-law stated that he knew of some apartments for rent and he knew the apartment manager. I got her number from him, called her that day, and I went to see the apartment that week. I knew I was going to take it because I had no more time to look for a place, and my children and I had over-stayed our welcome.

I realized that when things are going every which way in my life God was preparing me. My mind had to be renewed mentally to move on by myself, for the first time in 38 years. I never lived alone, and I never paid full rent by myself. When I agreed to take over a 12-month lease on my own, I was overjoyed and when fear of how was I about to do this on my own became a thought in my mind, I reminded myself of how much revenue I brought home and my first priority was home.

My mother and I still laugh at the day I received my keys to the place my family calls home. She said, "Y 'all had nothing, but y'all went to your new place like you guys had everything." My soul was tired. I do not have any bad habits. I work every day, sometimes two jobs. I obey the laws of the land and I am an excellent mother. My soul was very tired. That night, in that empty apartment, where we made pallets on the floor, was the best sleep I had in four years. The turning of the key meant wholeness and a peace-of-mind. We set up eventually the little things we did have and we lived knowing we all had a peace-of-mind.

Notes

Living Free Again

I told myself, "I believe in you, just live on purpose and live out your dreams." I could not cry out to another person, in reality everyone knew I was only human but they were trying to see how much I could take. I would never give the world the satisfaction of seeing me tired, but deep down my soul was tired. With every eviction I had to get rid of stuff, stuff that I held on to over the years as memories; looking back it was all a part of my healing process.

Damon did not completely understand the WOMAN he had. Year after year I stayed until my life became so unbearable that I had to walk away, leaving the only life I ever knew behind. The thought of walking away with nothing but the clothes on my back was not just a metaphor. It was my reality.

I left behind 20 years of memories, 20 years that my husband and I worked hard for, all left behind in a house or in the garbage. It made me think if I can leave behind 20 years of stuff and we still have each other, then we are on a journey to something amazing.

I started gathering my daily thoughts of me and telling myself daily I AM ENOUGH. Stuff can be replaced, but the only things that can ease the pain and humility of tragedy with one's life is when we get to the point of not holding it in and to the point where we understand those encounters do not define who we are, it is just some things we had to endure on our amazing journey through this life.

Family life was different for me but I knew life had to go on. I never really talked to people about my life and the things that were going on daily, because I never wanted sympathy, I just really needed people to understand that we have to live with our choices. I use to tell myself that wasn't my choice, but in fact, it was. I knew Damon used alcohol on a daily basis since he was about 15. I had an understanding of what alcoholism does to the person who uses it, but my firsthand experience in a marriage with an alcoholic showed me what alcoholism does to the families as well as the person addicted to the substance, which I now refer to as STRONGHOLD.

This stronghold came into our lives, people who hold each other to a higher standard, people who love God/The Most High and looked to his presence daily, people who walk through life adding to it not taking away from it; and it crippled us. It took away our power to understand one another as a family then after so many years of the repeatedly same outcome, it took away our powers to love the man who helped create our beautiful family and the man that was supposed to lead us. I never imagined that the man I knew and loved would ever be defeated by alcohol. He overcame so much in life previously.

Damon had literally been on his own since the age of 14, therefore, he lived every day in survival mode, and I was for sure that he could kick this habit. There was something about the alcohol that took total control over, and transformed, his mind into believing that all he needed was the STRONGHOLD.

It hurt so deep to know that I could never be more important to my husband than alcohol; to know that all our children were doing and accomplishing he never recognized as important enough to put that bottle down; and to know he'd never share moments of success with his children because of a STRONGHOLD.

Finding Me

I was now in the process of completely healing my heart so I could love again and become stronger and wiser than before. I would never exclude Damon from my life, I would be lying if I said the whole marriage was horrible, but I will say that I can never allow myself to go back to the life I had with him. I used to tell myself daily that none of this nightmare belonged to ME, when in fact, it was the life I chose.

I did not understand fully why I was in these tremendous life changing events happening in my life. Therefore, it was hard for me to understand the direction they were going to take me. Walking away from everything just to have peace; you're not only rebuilding your fall, but you also build character, love and respect for yourself.

When I ran to look for you that is when I found ME! It took me some time, but before I knew it I had let go. I now smile without reason and I am loving it. We ran from situations that we were afraid of because we did not understand that those are the moments in our lives we need to help us stand strong in the face of adversity. The character within myself was built, resistance was built and the discovery of self-love was built.

I faced every teardrop, I faced every emotion that I never let out and it felt great. I realized I was not this strong person that had to have a perfect life, I was human and it was time to face human emotions built up inside of me. We as humans are always running from our own selves and our needs until we have those moments in life where we are all we have and need. Not only did God turn our lives upside down but we both had to hit rock bottom to look up to see God was always right in the middle – we just pushed him out.

It is amazing how life events keep you on a path that was created just for you.

It may have just seemed like it was four years of a bad nightmare, but earlier events from our marriage prepared me for those four nightmarish years. Although I was never truly prepared for it. I can truly say did survive it. I always tried to drown myself in thoughts about what went wrong, how I could have fixed it, why I allowed Damon to drink and the disrespect.

Trust me, the more I thought about my circumstances and the ways it could have happened, the more I resented Damon and the less empathy in my heart I felt for him. I completely shut him out, which now that I sit here and write, it was a good thing. It gave me and him time to start healing and understanding what had taken place. I really pondered on two points from this situation. One was abandonment and the second one was illness, but both led me to FORGIVENESS.

Notes

I was so madly in love with Damon that the tragedy of those life events put a hole in my heart where he once resided. I mean, I went days without talking to him, I would never look at him; I just totally blocked Damon out of my life. I never could talk to anyone about how I was really feeling. Everyone assumed because I showed so much strength and ability to press through everything that came my way that I was fine. Deep down, a huge part of my 20 years of my living had come crumbling down. I was finally aware that I was broken.

I started to use my platforms on my social media sites to tell how I was feeling deep down inside. That seemed to help me cope with the PAIN that was not visible to the human eye, but it lay dormant inside of me. These posts allowed me to speak life back into my empty soul and allowed my FAITH in the MOST HIGH GOD to carry me through my long, lonely, lost days. I started cutting everyone around me out of my life, especially if they were a part of Damon.

Although I never talked to anyone concerning how I felt, confusion on the way I would express my feelings on my sites lead to misunderstanding of how I was coping with my life. I was never bashing anyone, I was telling pieces of my story through my lens. If Damon wanted a better story from me, he should've written on my heart differently.

I shut so many people out, and as I look back, it was the best way for me to gain my peace and wholeness back. I was so confused with life, I lived in a world with billions of people and I still thought no one was hearing my silent cries that I painted with every post shared on my sites. I now know I died, but was still living.

Abandonment ... I went through 20-plus years of having another human life by my side day and night. I could call any time of day or night and whatever I wanted or needed Damon would have gotten done. The very fact that Damon lived for his family after being a son that never knew his own biological father, was truly a beautiful sight to witness and a beautiful gift to my little family. It all was happening slowly, over a period of time. Damon was slowly drifting away from us, his family.

I am the type of person that watches over people's well-being, but to watch over your every move and what you are buying and doing with your time, will take away too much of my time. Over the years I gradually became only focused on where my life was headed. It may sound selfish, but I was tired after continually talking, giving resources, listening attentively and being very understanding for that 20 years of marriage.

The results that were being produced were becoming a pattern. He thought if he pretended to listen to me that I would go on about my life. By now I felt my words and actions were empty to his ears and his lifestyle was my witness, therefore, I began building me a life without Damon.

I never believed or could understand why my plans and dreams for my future did not have Damon in them. It was so scary, heartbreaking and lonely to think someone I damn near grew up with would not be a part of my future. As I told him on a few occasions that I stopped seeing him in my future, he would brush it off and always stated he can stop drinking when he wanted to. That was the furthest statement from the truth. The truth was, he was never going to leave his surroundings and he found comfort and life in alcohol. Damon had a real sickness and no matter what I said or showed him, Damon feeding his sickness was the only thing he knew, he would never understand my actions were out of love. Damon had a family, God gave him everything he didn't have in us, but his sickness would not allow him to see his blessings.

Notes

Illness

The time I spent resenting Damon and completely ignoring his existence was the time I had come to realize that he was SICK ... I racked my brain, I researched alcoholism and I looked back over our life and put his patterns together. I finally came to realize that this sickness had a stronghold on Damon and that sickness took over the man I once called my husband, the father to my children.

The Damon I met and married would have never allowed his family to fall apart and not be the provider for his family. I witnessed how alcohol can take the strongest amongst us all and reduce their lives to pieces. I watched this sickness make a man have no care for another human life. The only thing he wanted to know was how and where his next drink was coming from.

In my eyes, Damon didn't see us as his family anymore, we had become a resource to him. I also realized that I had been his enabler. I was always catching him in the middle of his fall and no matter how much I tried, I realized until he wanted different for his life then there was nothing I could do to save him. The sickness of alcoholism had taken over his cognitive skills to think logically and rationally. I was truly alone.

I am so scared, I don't want to do this thing called life alone. We set out on path together and 20 years later we stand alone. How can a substance of liquid dissolve a lifetime of planned happiness? We had dreams of seeing the world together, but as I stood behind you taking this picture, this would be our last view of the world together.

We painted remarkable pictures under these skies and no matter what happens in life I know you will always be looking over your children, grandchildren and me, as we are doing the same for you.

I am scared out of my mind but after I realized that you had no control over your sickness, I started making sure you knew that I forgave you. I had some soul searching of my own to do.

I leaned on God and his unchanging hand. I found it in myself to start loving me as much as I loved Damon and our children. I witnessed the pain he was in and realized he had no control over it. I finally came to an understanding that it was just how the tables in Damon's life had turned and that I was a big part of that turn.

Forgiveness

I wish I can tell you it was all a dream, but God knew the plan for your life before you were formed in your mother's womb. Our children and I had an inside look at the destruction of alcoholism, and although life as we knew it had forever changed, on December 17, 2018, we knew in order to heal, it had to start with FORGIVENESS.

DAMON, I forgive you. My children's father was battling end-stage Alcohol Liver Cirrhosis. The doctors of Damon's liver team did not tell us the exact day we would no longer have him in our lives, but we knew whatever time we had left we were going to spend it cherishing one another. I could not carry non-forgiveness in my heart, so I let it all go and forgave Damon.

This STRONG man had been by my side for over 20 years. A stronghold of alcohol took over him and he became sick. I would never hold that against him. That is not the young man I met and fell completely in love with; those traits are the outcome of dependency. I FORGIVE YOU. MAY YOUR SOUL REST IN PEACE . Damon died on December 03, 2019.

It took some soul searching, a lot of spiritual growth and unexplained wisdom for me to truly understand that our life had to happen this way. The life I valued and cherished so deeply had to be on display for the world to see. There was no way we could have taken all that had happened to us and push it under the rug. There would not have been healing, forgiveness and awareness of alcoholism destroying not only the person who is addicted to the chemical but everyone around that is near and dear to their heart.

When we are young, we feel invincible to everything. Having fun partying with lots of drugs and alcohol seems harmless and the way the youth express themselves.

I am here to tell you that harmless drinking leads to a daily devotion to the bottle that becomes a stronghold over your life. Is it really worth losing everything? Everything to a person prior to chemical dependency on alcohol means nothing to them in an alcoholic's state of mind. In most cases, the only thing they are buying with their money is alcohol. That is all they see and all they know. It is not until they break completely down and the only person left as they reach up is the person they hurt deeply for years.

An alcoholic never knows the pain they are causing because in actuality they are too sick and mentally unable to feel empathy for the persons in their life that love them and want them to get better. Once they realize that the person or people who love them have moved on with life, it becomes an even harder reality for the alcoholic to face sober. I don't think the effects of this stronghold really end.

Damon was torn between living the rest of his life alone or going back to alcohol which he knew would result badly. He would tell me all the time, "I am dealing with a lot." My answer back to him would always be, "I know you are, but I have to keep living my life, without you this time."

Living Life on My Own

It's been hard for me because all I knew and all I cared for was Damon and our children. I knew my life was changing during my nightmare, but these next steps were going to determine if I was going to float through life or drown.

Damon could not help me financially and he was barely holding on mentally, but I never let him suffer alone. Even though we were separated, I took care of Damon. He told me all the time that my children and I are all he knows. It's easy to toss someone to the side, put them away because your life is so busy another person with a sickness would slow you down.

It's very easy to turn your back on people who failed to love, cherish, and adore you. What we do for those people when the world is not looking helps one know what kind of heart/character one has. As a mother, role model, child of The Most High God, how could I allow myself to mistreat someone that an addiction took over? I was determined to love Damon through his pain and finding himself again.

Damon would always say "I am dealing with a lot." I kind of understood where he was coming from. That is exactly how I felt eight years prior, when my whole world that I knew came crashing down. I never would tell him that; I just did as God instructed us to do; love our neighbors as we love ourselves.

Never Judge a Book

I am a walking example of never judging a book by its cover. I would sometimes wonder, WHY ME, FATHER GOD ... and I will always come back to the same answer. WHY NOT YOU. I am just a vessel used by God to make an impact on Earth and I vow to never let my circumstances determine who God created me to be.

Damon got a tattoo on his right forearm, over 15 years ago, in which he chose to portray me as his angel. I have never seen myself as anything much more than Robin, and to be someone's earthly angel was an honor.

I could have turned my back and walked away, but I knew this period of my life was much bigger than me. I was building character and substance to sustain. As I stated earlier, I was very scared, I was terrified of the unknown. Who will love me, who will take care of me and my children, who will protect, guide and always look over us?

In the midst of my STORM, I met God for myself. In His words, He said, "I will never leave you or forsake you, even in the ends of time." I am standing on His words because they have never come back void. Alcoholism does not just have an effect on the person who abuses it, but it destroys everything and everyone attached to the person who has the addiction.

My mom told me something when I was in my youth. She had little sayings that would play over and over in your head until you reached their meaning. Her words exactly were, "Our habits is what kills us." That is something for a 15-year-old to think about. I had no idea what a habit was; all I wanted to do was play sports and hang out with my friends. Now, 25 years later, I have seen what it is when a habit has only taken away the user's ability to live a long life and be able to live out their dreams. That habit also took away the user's loved ones' ability to thrive during their time with the abuser.

My dreams were put on hold and put me into a mental state of darkness. I was trying to help someone who didn't know he needed help, and in the process, I was losing everything we worked so hard for in the process. What I have learned is that our actions do not just affect us, but they affect the welfare of all the people around them.

I never knew that what we do affects others until it was in my own backyard. It was like a nightmare that just would not stop. Our life would hit rock bottom then we would come up little bit; then rock bottom again. At some point I just couldn't keep up with that roller coaster lifestyle anymore. People reach out for help when it is too late to turn around the damage they did to themselves internally and the damage they put on another person's heart.

No matter how much I think I should be upset with Damon, I cannot. He was a young black boy trapped in society's norm of children in urban communities. His view of life was what he eventually became a part of, and it was not changing his perception of things. Damon was trapped mentally in a cycle where all he knew was to wake up daily and take a drink, that would help him function throughout the day.

I, at one time, even told myself, "Well, I know that is how he gets his day started," and then would convince myself it was right. I take my part of the blame but I also know someone who has an addiction will only change when they see fit to do it for themselves.

That is why I picked my head up from self-pity, self-doubt and self-hatred toward my circumstances. I told myself I am not that. I was crippled with blind faith and love in a man that took over my ability to see the bigger picture. I left it all behind me. I lost everything but my sanity and with that truth I started to rebuild my life. We can get material things back but how can we get back our right mind after we've lost it?

Notes

Desiring More

I don't look at the people in my life as a half-full or half-empty glass of something. I look at them as if that is all they could give me. When I start desiring more, I have to go get it instead of trying to beat it out of someone when that is all they can give me.

I knew Damon was so used to the 17-25-year-old me, but the truth was that I was changing. Mind, Body, and Soul. I had become this woman right in front of his eyes, and but the stronghold the substance had on him wouldn't allow him to even notice me. He avoided me because he didn't want me to ask him any questions concerning anything and I avoided him because I didn't want to see what he had withered down to.

When I walked completely away in 2016, I walked into a new Robin. Guilt, shame, and hurt were no longer going to live within me. I am so determined and focused to live the second half of my life FREE from any judgments or stipulations that will hold me back from soaring to my fullest potential. It is not what we do for people when the world is watching us, it is what we do for them when no one is watching us. Damon was still taking care of the children and me, Damon was still a major part of our lives and he would always be my family.

What I faced gave me a very humbling soul and a beautiful outlook on life for the people in it. I cried many nights and I still cry at night. The difference between the cries of yesterday and today is that I feel God's presence within me and I fall quickly to sleep. I also know today that every situation has an end date so I refuse to let the pressures of life stop me from growing. I am a rose who grew from concrete and turned all the negatives into positives. I look at everything now as what if it was me. I would want someone to take me in and help me. Damon just had a stronghold on him, there was nothing more or less I could do.

God's Word instructed me to plant a mustard seed of faith in Damon and He would do the rest. Am I my brother's keeper as I would so often use jokingly as a teenager? Today, as I stand as a mother of four at her prime age of 42, yes I am, and it is my duty as a child of the Most High God to love and take care of my brothers and sisters.

God will turn your whole life around just to get you on the path that was created just for you. We all have a journey and a destination; how we get there one may never know. My suggestion, through it all, is run your race. The more you give of yourself through your adversities, the more blessed you will be and the more strength you will gain to endure to the end. I am living life on my own terms now, cautious not to get thrown into a new nightmare. Looking to the Creator with every step I make and holding on to his words to get me through the tears that sneak down my cheeks.

Damon, your memory will forever live on through all your loved ones.

Made in the USA
Middletown, DE
30 March 2022